GW00993567

THE BIG BOSS WHO MAKES A PACKET
OUT OF PROTECTION

RAVE BOOKS

Big Bad Dom ran a protection racket.

For a price, he would make sure you stayed out of trouble.

That's business – and he was a businessman.

Big Bad Dom was smart.
He knew it wasn't safe out there.

Guys couldn't trust Babes.
Babes couldn't trust Guys.

You didn't know who was carrying.

If you were in with the wrong people,
you were gonna get hit.

So you would talk to Big Bad Dom first –
about protection.

He was the best there was.

It all started with the barbers.

Big Bad Dom just walked in there, opened up his case and the joint went quiet.

"Just pay for a little protection,
and you'll be secure this weekend,"
said Big Bad Dom.

There was no stopping Big Bad Dom.

Within weeks everybody was into protection – whether they liked it or not.

It was like the whole city had exploded.

If you had a shooter, then you were a target.

So, you talked to Big Bad Dom.

He told you the cost. And you did a deal.

That way you knew you'd be all right tonight.

Big Bad Dom always had you
just where he wanted you.

If you played dirty, or took a risk,
he was on to you, real fast.

And if you played the game,
he protected your interests.

"Hey! My ladies wanna taste of the action," shouted Dolly Hardon.

Dolly's ladies worked the club scene.

"How many guys you got comin' regularly?" asked Big Bad Dom.

"We all gotta handful," Dolly replied.

Big Bad Dom flicked open his case.

The ladies gasped.

"I want each and everyone of you to know that I mean business," he said firmly.

"You're gonna get guys mouthin' off that they're real good. But now I'm around, you don't have to swallow any more of their rubbish."

"You tell 'em they either wrap up... or talk to me."

At the petrol station Big Bad Dom hit on Phyllis Pumper.

"When you're serving customers 24-hours you need protecting," he stated.

"And if I say no?" said Phyllis.

"Then you're gonna end up with a stiff on your hands," warned Big Bad Dom.

Next Big Bad Dom nobbled the chemist.

"You wanna see your mates, then you're
gonna have to play safe and pay up,"
said Big Bad Dom.

He gave the chemist a hard time.

And left him with a mass of black and blue ribs.

Big Bad Dom burst through a back room door.

"TIME TO CLEAN UP!" he shouted.

Everybody hit the deck.

"OK guys," said Big Bad Dom. "There's been a lotta cheatin' goin' on... and I don't like that kinda gamblin'."

"We weren't doin' nothin'," somebody said.

"Well I'm gonna make sure you play your cards right in future," replied Big Bad Dom.

"If you wanna little fun and games,
then you do it my way – the Dom way."

"That's the only way to be sure you don't end up
with a big problem."

They all started to move towards him.

Big Bad Dom opened up his case…

And one by one he let them have it.

"I hear you worked over the casino last night," said Shorty Piece, the journalist.

"Listen," said Big Bad Dom, "I made those guys an offer they couldn't refuse."

"You get my story on your front page, and you won't be havin' a circulation problem!"

Everybody read the story in the press.

The Mayor, the politicians, the police.

Then the screaming really started.

Who was this Big Boss who ran a
protection racket in their city?

Big Bad Dom was a wanted man.

Big Bad Dom was up against it in a back alley.

"Assume the position," said the first policewoman.

"Spread 'em," said the second.

"We're gonna frisk ya," said the third.

"Is this what you're after?" asked Big Bad Dom.

Before they could answer he had grabbed his case, and flicked the catch...

"Feelin' lucky?... then make your choice,"
said Big Bad Dom.

"Cos you just bought into my protection racket!"